MEDIEVAL SCOTLAND

RICHARD DARGIE

Explore Scottish History is packed with historical evidence  to help you discover how Scotland's people lived in the past. It also includes links to the Heinemann Explore website and CD-ROM ⊙.

Heinemann
LIBRARY

H www.heinemann.co.uk/library
Visit our website to find out more information about Heinemann Library books.

To order:
☎ Phone 44 (0) 1865 888066
📄 Send a fax to 44 (0) 1865 314091
💻 Visit the Heinemann Library Bookshop at www.heinemann.co.uk/library to browse our catalogue and order online.

First published in Great Britain by Heinemann Library, Halley Court, Jordan Hill, Oxford OX2 8EJ, a division of Reed Educational and Professional Publishing Ltd. Heinemann is a registered trademark of Reed Educational & Professional Publishing Ltd.

OXFORD MELBOURNE AUCKLAND JOHANNESBURG BLANTYRE GABORONE IBADAN PORTSMOUTH (NH) USA CHICAGO

Designed by Celia Floyd
Originated by Dot Gradations
Printed by Wing King Tong in Hong Kong

06 05 04 03 02
10 9 8 7 6 5 4 3 2 1
ISBN 0 431 14522 9 (hardback)

06 05 04 03 02
10 9 8 7 6 5 4 3 2 1
ISBN 0 431 14523 7 (paperback)

British Library Cataloguing in Publication Data

Dargie, Richard
  Medieval Scotland. – (Explore Scottish history)
  1. Scotland – History – 1057-1603 – Juvenile literature
  I. Title
  941.1'02

Acknowledgements

The Publishers would like to thank the following for permission to reproduce photographs:

AKG photo pp13, 24, Art Archive p21, Bridgeman Art Library p23, Corbis p17, Heritage Image Partnership pp28 (British Library), 29 (British Library), Hulton Getty pp6, 16, Mary Evans Picture Library pp7, 18, National Library of Scotland Map Library p10, National Trust for Scotland p11, Scotland in Focus pp5 (J Smith), 8 (Willbir), 12 (R Schofield), 15, 19 (Willbir) 20 (Willbir), 22 (J Smith), 26, SCRAN pp9, 14 Timepix (Mansell) p25.

Cover photograph reproduced with permission of The Art Archive.

Our thanks to Ian Hall of the University of St Andrews for his comments during the writing of this book.

Every effort has been made to contact copyright holders of any material reproduced in this book. Any omissions will be rectified in subsequent printings if notice is given to the Publisher.

Any words appearing in the text in bold, **like this**, are explained in the glossary.

Contents

The people of Alba

Before the year AD 1000, most people in Scotland lived in the kingdom of Alba. The people of Alba spoke **Gaelic** and were mostly peasants who lived in the countryside. They lived in villages called **clachans** and built oblong houses with stone walls packed with mud and dried leaves.

The people of Alba made their living from farming, fishing and hunting. They grew crops such as barley and oats, but most of their wealth came from herds of cattle and flocks of sheep. There was little trade in Scotland at this time. There were few coins and people just bartered or exchanged goods. Most villagers paid their rent by offering food to the landowner. They made their own clothes by spinning and weaving a rough yarn.

There were no large towns but there were a few important settlements. The king often stayed at the walled 'touns' of Perth and Forteviot. Small towns were also growing around the ports at Aberdeen and Dundee, and there were important churches at Dunkeld and St Andrews.

The land was governed by the Mormaers or Earls. These nobles protected the local people in return for their loyalty in time of war. Each Mormaer was in charge of a district. When the king died, the Mormaers met to choose a new king. They usually picked a noble who had proved he was a good leader and a strong warrior in battle. The new king was announced at a ceremony at Scone in Perthshire where he had to sit upon the sacred Stone of Destiny.

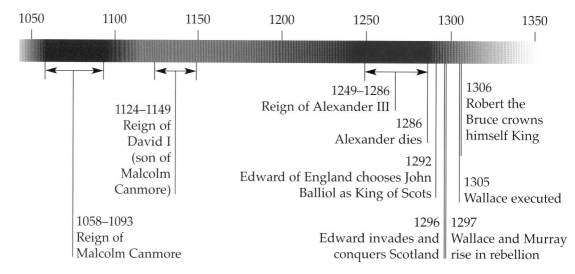

1050 — 1100 — 1150 — 1200 — 1250 — 1300 — 1350

1124–1149
Reign of David I (son of Malcolm Canmore)

1249–1286
Reign of Alexander III

1286
Alexander dies

1306
Robert the Bruce crowns himself King

1292
Edward of England chooses John Balliol as King of Scots

1305
Wallace executed

1058–1093
Reign of Malcolm Canmore

1296
Edward invades and conquers Scotland

1297
Wallace and Murray rise in rebellion

Lookout towers such as this one at Brechin gave defenders warning if enemies approached.

After AD 1000 many things began to change in Scotland. The kingdom's name changed from Alba to Scotia. Towns and trade began to grow. The kings of Scotland began to rule the country in new, different ways. Many of these new ways of life came from the **Normans**. They were a strong well-organized people from northern France. In 1066 a Norman army invaded and conquered England. They did not conquer Scotland but many Normans settled here, bringing their experience and ideas.

From a Norman chronicle written in 1072

"King William led a great Norman army against Scotland. Malcolm collected his men and came against the Normans. The two kings met each other at Abernethy, their barons spoke a great deal and the kings came to an agreement. All the Scots thanked God."

"Alba or Scotia has pretty, rich lands with green meadows, fertile for growing corn and barley and pease but not suited for wine and oil. It is full of pasture grass for cattle and wool-bearing sheep and rich in horses. The rivers, lakes and seas are rich in fish and birds of many kinds."

From the Chronicle of John of Fordoun

Exploring further

The Heinemann Explore CD-ROM will give you information about the Middle Ages. From the Contents screen you can click on the blue words to find out about Scotland and the wider world.

Scots and Normans

Macbeth was the last of the old **Gaelic** kings of Alba. He died in AD 1057. The new king of Scotland was Malcolm III called Canmore or the Great Chieftain. Malcolm, his wife Margaret and their son David I respected their **Norman** neighbours in England but they also knew that the Normans were powerful and dangerous warriors. Malcolm and Margaret set out to change and strengthen their kingdom, often copying Norman ideas.

This illustration of David I and Malcolm III is the earliest surviving drawing of a Scottish king.

Unlike the Alban kings who spoke Gaelic, Malcolm also spoke Inglis or English, and French – the language of the Normans. He moved his capital from Perthshire to a new fortress at Dunfermline. This was protected from attack by the river Forth and from here he could send ships to trade overseas.

Margaret became Queen of Scotland in AD 1070. She asked monks from England and Europe to come to Scotland and build an abbey at Dunfermline. She paid for ferries to carry thousands of **pilgrims** across the Forth each year to the shrine of St Andrew in Fife.

Norman knights on horseback were fast and well protected war machines.

Malcolm and Margaret had six sons. The youngest was David who became king in 1124 and was one of the greatest kings in Scottish history. David built a strong army, led by well-trained Norman knights. He invited them into Scotland and gave them rich lands along the border with England. The families of these knights protected Scotland for centuries.

David also knew that Scotland needed more **merchants** and craftsmen. He founded many **burghs** or trading towns and ordered the first minting of silver coins in Scotland. He allowed the burghs to hold markets and fairs. Merchants from all over Europe began to come to Scotland to buy and sell goods.

After Malcolm came to the throne, the old Gaelic Mormaers lost their power. They could no longer elect their king – instead the throne passed to the next in line. They also lost their power in local government. Now a sheriff ran every part of the kingdom. His job was to make sure that the king's law was obeyed. Many of the sheriffs were Norman knights.

Norman surnames found in Scotland:

Barclay: Bisset: Bruce: Cumming: Fraser: Grant: Hay: Landles: Lindsay: Menzies: Montgomery: Somerville: Stewart: Sinclair.

Exploring further – The Norman conquest

Use the CD-ROM to discover more about the Norman Invasion of England. Follow this path: Exploring the Wider World > Focus On: Britain 1066–1500 Then click on either The Battle of Hastings or The Norman conquest.

Scottish knights and castles

After AD 1100 there were new **Norman** lords in many parts of Scotland. They were given land or estates by the king and allowed to build a castle to protect their land and goods. David I gave large grants of land to two of his most trusted Norman friends, Robert de Brus and Walter le Steward. In time their families both became royal houses of Scotland.

The first castles were simple towers made of timber. They were usually built on an earthen hill or motte. The stables and workshops were built in a nearby lower courtyard or bailey. Many of these motte and bailey castles were built in Scotland by Norman lords. Later these wooden forts were replaced by stronger stone castles.

A stone keep or tower was built on top of the motte and bailey at Castle Duffus in Moray.

The Norman lords ran their estates in a new way. They divided up their land and gave each part to a loyal knight or soldier. In return, these men promised to fight for their lord in time of war. The knights then divided the land up again. They shared it out amongst their tenant farmers who had to give the knight food and other services. In return, he protected them. Each piece of land was called a feu. As a result, this way of running the country was called feudalism.

Norman knights were highly-skilled warriors who fought on horseback. Every farmer in Scotland also had to be ready to fight for his lord or for the king as a foot soldier. Men between 16 and 60 had to supply their own weapons and armour and prove that they could use them. The local sheriff made sure that this law was obeyed by inspecting the men on parade twice a year at a wapinschaw or weapon showing.

The kings of Scotland used these troops to win back land from the **Norse** and the English. William the Lion was a warrior king who fought the Norse in the northern counties of Ross and Caithness. He also invaded northern England several times. William was the first Scottish king to use the yellow and red Lion Rampant as his flag.

The Lion Rampant.
This red standing lion on a yellow flag became the Royal Standard of Scotland in the 12th Century.

From an early Act of the Scottish Parliament

"In time of war, each man shall get a thick leather jacket, a helmet, a good spear and a sword. And the king orders that each sheriff will check these things at a wapinschaw"

Exploring further – Medieval Knights

Castles and knights could be found in other parts of Britain and Europe during the Middle Ages. The CD-ROM looks at how medieval knights lived. Follow this path: Exploring the Wider World > Focus On: Medieval Knights Click on the different topic headings to find out more.

Life in the burghs

In Scotland in the Middle Ages you could only buy and sell goods in a **burgh**. At first, these were small villages where **merchants** stored their goods. By 1300 many of the burghs had grown into rich and important towns like Berwick and Aberdeen.

 This is a 1580 drawing of the burgh of St Andrews. The three-storey timber houses were built along the High Street with long strips of land called **tofts** behind them.

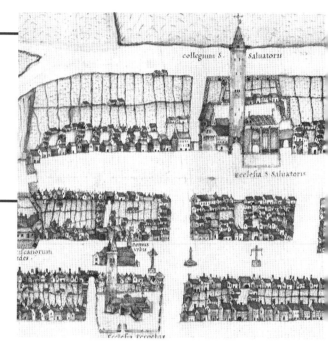

Most burghs had a **Mercat Cross** to show where the market was held. The **Tron** or public weighing scales also stood here. Many burghs had a tolbooth or tower where valuable things, and prisoners, were kept under lock and key. Burghs were sometimes attacked by local lords who wanted their riches, so they were usually protected by a wooden **stockade** and a moat or ditch.

The burgesses or burgh merchants had special permission from the king to hold fairs and markets. These rights were written down in the Burgh Charter. It was an important document so it was usually kept safe in a locked chest in the tolbooth. The burgh was run by the **Provost** and the burgesses who sat on the Town Council. They made laws and sentenced criminals.

 From the Burgh Charter of Aberdeen

"Robert, King of Scots, grants to the burgesses of Aberdeen, mills, fishings, the right to charge tolls and other privileges. In return the burgesses will pay 213 pounds, 6 shillings and 8 pence."

Craftsmen had to join a **guild** like the Souters (shoemakers), Saddlers and Skinners. The guilds set the price of things in the burgh and made sure that goods were of high quality. Only members of guilds like the Bakers, Millers and Butchers could sell food at the burgh market. Each guild had a **Deacon** who watched over the apprentices who were learning their craft. He also judged the masterpiece, which they had to make to show that they were good enough to join the guild.

The burgh came alive on market day and the annual fair. Glasgow's fair lasted for eight days. People came from miles around to see the stalls and booths set up by travelling hawkers and pedlars. There were also jugglers, acrobats and dancing bears.

 The Mercat Cross, like this one at Culross, was an important meeting place for merchants and craftsmen.

Exploring further – Daily life

The Digging Deeper section of the CD-ROM allows you to find out more about the topics that interest you: Digging Deeper > Medieval Britain 1066 to 1485 gives details about daily life in Scotland and other parts of Britain.

Life in Dunfermline Abbey

Dunfermline Abbey was one of the richest monasteries in Scotland. It was founded by Queen Margaret in the 1070s. The monks who lived at Dunfermline followed the Rule of St Benedict and took vows to live in silence. Over three hundred years they built a magnificent abbey, that was one of the finest buildings in the kingdom. Queen Margaret and many Scottish kings were buried there.

Kings and queens founded abbeys for many reasons. They knew that the hard-working monks would be prosperous. They traded with other abbeys in Europe and brought wealth to Scotland. The monks were educated and often built schools for the sons of lords and knights. This meant that Scotland's leaders were well educated. Founding an abbey was also a holy act. Margaret and her son David hoped this would find favour with God.

Next to the church were the dormitories where the monks slept and the refectory where they ate. There was a separate house for the abbot and a guesthouse for visitors such as the king. Many abbeys also had worksheds, mills and barns where the wealth of the monastery was made and stored. Some monks worked in the **scriptorium** where they copied and illustrated holy books such as the Bible.

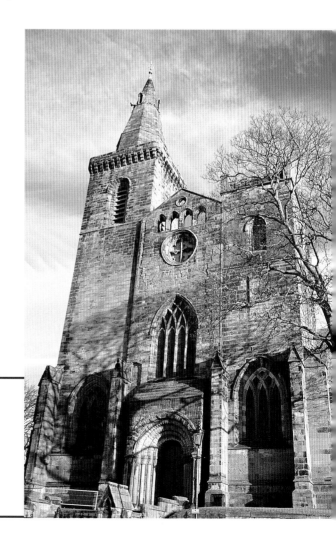

 The main building at Dunfermline was the high abbey church. Benedictine monks had to worship in the church seven times every day.

Monasteries and abbeys were not just important churches. The monks were often businessmen and had skills in farming and trade. Wool from the Border abbeys at Melrose and Jedburgh was sent by ship to European cities where it was turned into fine cloth. The hard work of monks added greatly to Scotland's prosperity.

At Paisley Abbey **archaeologists** found a blocked drain full of rubbish left by the monks hundreds of years before. They found dice, game pieces and two slates with music scratched on them. Food remains in the drain showed that the monks used expensive spices such as nutmeg and ginger to hide the taste of bad meat. The rubbish also contained traces of medicine made from herbs like hemlock, which was used as a painkiller.

Benedictine monks, such as the ones who lived at Dunfermline Abbey, followed a strict daily routine of prayer, manual labour and study.

David I founds an abbey in Fife in 1135

"Know all men that I, David King of Scots, grant to the monks of St Andrews the island of Lochleven, so that they may set up an order of monks there and live according to their rules...."

Exploring further – The Church

During the Middle Ages, the Church in England and Scotland was ruled by the Pope in Rome. Discover more on the CD-ROM by following this path: Digging Deeper > Medieval Britain 1066–1485 > Church and king.

Life in Dirleton Castle

Dirleton Castle was one of the mightiest fortresses in Europe. It was built around 1240 by the Baron John de Vaux, who had rich lands in France as well as Scotland. His new castle at Dirleton was designed by the best **masons** in the country. It had to be difficult to capture, for it stood on the road from England to Edinburgh. Any invading army from the south would be forced to attack or **besiege** Dirleton. It was one of the keys to the kingdom of Scotland.

Castles like Dirleton had many uses. It was the home of the baron and his family so some rooms had to be comfortable. There were also sumptuous guestrooms in case the king came to stay. The baron used the castle's **Great Hall** as a courtroom when he judged the quarrels brought to him. Deep below were the pits where criminals and prisoners were kept. About a hundred people lived and worked as servants in the castle and the nearby farms. This community was fed by the castle's kitchens and sheltered by its walls.

This illustration shows how the inside of Dirleton Castle might have looked. Castle estates had to provide food and fuel for the lord, his family and the surrounding community.

Above all, the castle folk had to be ready for war. The Constable was in charge of the soldiers. In time of war there were probably around 80 fighting men at Dirleton. Some had special skills such as firing the castle's war engines. In the courtyard was the blacksmith's forge where armour was toughened and weapon points sharpened. The Marshall's job was to make sure that the horses of the Baron and his knights were ready for battle. If war threatened, the Pantler had to gather in all the food from the farms and store it in the castle cellars.

Scotland was a kingdom full of castles. Some defended Scotland's southern border. Others in the west were built to protect Scotland's coasts from the **Norse**. Many of Scotland's castles survive as ruins but others have disappeared completely. The castles in Glasgow and Aberdeen were taken to pieces by the townsfolk who used the stones to build houses and streets. All that survives is the evidence of street names such as Castlegate.

Dirleton was defended by a moat, a drawbridge and vast rounded towers.

From a Scottish chronicle

"...The plague broke out in Edinburgh so the King rode the same day to Dirleton Castle to a sumptuous banket [banquet] prepared by the Earl, and the King remained at Dirleton for twelve days...."

Exploring further – Key people

The Biographies section of the CD-ROM will tell you more about famous people from medieval Scotland, including John de Vaux and many of Scotland's kings. Click on their names to read about these people.

The Wars of Independence: the realm without a king

Alexander III was a wise king who ruled Scotland well for 37 years. He won back lands from the **Norse** but made sure that his kingdom was at peace. Scotland prospered but Alexander left no direct heir to the throne. His two sons died before him. When Alexander fell to his death from the cliffs at Kinghorn in Fife in 1286, his only heir was his three-year-old granddaughter, Princess Margaret of Norway.

From a letter written by Alexander III

"No one has a right to homage from me for my kingdom of Scotland, for I hold it only from God."

The job of ruling Scotland was given to six important nobles called the Guardians, until Margaret was old enough to travel to her kingdom. In 1290 she sailed across the North Sea, but at Orkney she fell mysteriously ill and died. Now there was no heir to the Scottish Crown.

Edward I was the powerful King of England. He believed that he had the right to choose Scotland's next king. The Scots did not agree with this but they did want Edward to help them. There were thirteen Scottish nobles claiming that they should be the next King of Scotland. The two main rivals were John Balliol and Robert de Brus or Bruce, both rich nobles with many armed supporters. If it helped to avoid a **civil war**, most Scots were happy that Edward chose their next king.

The reign of Alexander III was viewed as a golden age by Scots caught up in the long conflict with England after his tragic death in 1286.

In 1291 Edward met the Scottish nobles at Berwick Castle to judge the claims of the two competitiors. He chose John Balliol but made John swear an oath of loyalty to him as overlord of Scotland. This made John look weak in the eyes of the Scots. When John did stand up to Edward in 1295, the English king invaded Scotland the following year.

Edward captures Edinburgh Castle

"Edward went to Edinburgh and there he ordered siege engines called trebuchets to be set up casting stones into the castle day and night, and on the fifth day the Scots came out and spoke of peace......"

Edward's powerful army quickly captured the main castles in Scotland. The Scottish nobles surrendered to him. The Stone of Destiny was taken from Scone to London, and placed under the English throne at Westminster. All the seals and special symbols of the Scottish king were destroyed. King John Balliol was replaced by an English governor. Edward ordered that Scotland was never to be called a kingdom again.

For seven hundred years, the Stone of Destiny lay under the English throne in Westminster Abbey.

Exploring further – Edward I

Follow this path on the CD-ROM to read about Edward I of England and his involvement with Scotland's history: Biographies > Edward I of England
When you have found the information about Edward, click on the picture on the left of the screen to make it bigger and find out what it shows.

Wallace and Murray: defenders of Scotland

In 1296 Edward I quickly conquered Scotland. Castles were captured and the Scottish nobles were defeated in battle at Dunbar. They were made to swear oaths of loyalty to Edward. The English king set out to destroy all signs of Scotland's independence. He ordered that Scotland be called a 'lordship' rather than a kingdom. When King John Balliol surrendered to Edward, the crown was torn from his head and he was taken to prison in London.

Edward was called 'The Hammer of the Scots'. However he had not conquered the people of Scotland. The ordinary folk hated him, and the soldiers whom he left to police their land. They especially hated Edward's **Treasurer** in Scotland, Hugh de Cressingham, who collected taxes from the Scots.

In May 1297 the Scots found two new leaders in their fight against the invader. William Wallace was a knight who had lands in Elderslie near Paisley. A legend says that the English burned his house and murdered his wife. In revenge, Wallace slew the English governor of Lanark. We do know that Wallace was declared an outlaw by the English. Throughout 1297 he and his men attacked English officials and stirred up resistance against Edward. In the north of Scotland, Andrew Murray organized an army and began to recapture land and castles taken by Edward. For the first time, the Scottish nation were united against a common enemy.

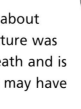

 There are many legends about William Wallace. This picture was painted long after his death and is just one idea of what he may have looked like.

The Scots ran down from Abbey Craig (the hill with the tower) when they saw the English army crossing Stirling Bridge.

In September 1297 Wallace and Murray met a larger English force at Stirling Bridge. The Scots chose their ground well, rushing down upon the enemy as they crossed the river Forth. The English were badly defeated, and Cressingham's hated corpse was skinned by the victorious Scots. Sadly, Andrew Murray died of his wounds but he and Wallace had shown that the Scots could defend their homeland.

Wallace was named Guardian of Scotland but soon had to flee to Europe when Edward himself led a huge army against him in 1298. In 1305 Wallace was betrayed and taken to London where he was charged with treason. He was hung, drawn and quartered and his limbs were put on display at towns across Scotland.

From a letter written by Wallace and Murray in 1298

"Andrew of Moray and William Wallace, leaders of the army of the Kingdom of Scotland proclaim that, thanks be to God, Scotland is recovered by war from the power of the English....."

Exploring further – Looking at wars

The CD-ROM includes pictures of medieval armies. These tell us about what they wore and the weapons they used. Follow this path: Pictures > Medieval knights Click on a picture to make it bigger and to read a caption telling you what it shows.

Bruce and Bannockburn

Edward thought that Scotland would accept his rule now that Wallace was dead. He was wrong for the Scots found a new leader in Robert the Bruce. Bruce was an important noble with lands and castles in the south west of Scotland. His grandfather had claimed the Scottish throne in 1291 but Edward chose Balliol instead.

Bruce had lands in England as well and he even fought for Edward against William Wallace. However, in 1306 Bruce rode to Scone with his knights and placed the crown of Scotland on his own head. At Greyfriars Kirk in Dumfries, he slew his main rival John Comyn, the Lord of Badenoch.

Bruce's first task was to make all Scots accept him as their king. He lost two battles at Methven and Dalry and had to go into hiding on Rathlin Island off the coast of Ireland. Legend says that it was here that Bruce watched a spider struggling to climb up to its web. The spider inspired Bruce to carry on his war against Edward.

Between 1308 and 1314, almost all of Scotland's castles were recaptured by the Scots. By 1314, only Stirling Castle remained in English hands. The English Governor agreed to hand the castle over to the Scots if no English army came to relieve him by Midsummer Day.

The new king of England, Edward II, marched north to Stirling Castle with a vast army of almost 25,000 men. This forced Bruce to meet the English in an open battle. Bruce had a much smaller army, so he had to choose the right place to attack.

 This modern statue commemorates the Scottish victory at the Battle of Bannockburn in June 1314.

Medieval battles, like Bannockburn, were messy and bloody affairs where men fought hand to hand.

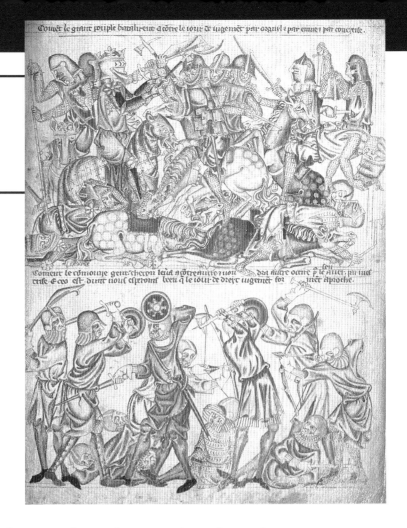

The night before the battle of Bannockburn, Bruce's men are said to have touched the **brecbannoch**, the casket that contained the holy bones of St Columba. At dawn, Bruce rode out to look at the battlefield and was attacked by Sir Henry de Bohun, the English champion. Bruce slew his foe and the spirits of the Scottish army rose.

The battle became a slaughter. The English knights were forced into the marshy ground beside the 'Bannock' burn. Soon this ditch was full of English dead. Edward fled south to Berwick, chased by Scottish horsemen.

Bruce's speech to his men at Bannockburn

"Those English barons you can see before you, clad in mail, are bent upon destroying me and my kingdom, nay our whole nation. They glory in their warhorses and equipment. They do not believe that we can survive. This day, Saint Andrew shall fight with us for the honour of our country and the nation."

Exploring further – Robert the Bruce

The Digging Deeper section of the CD-ROM takes a detailed look at the life of Robert the Bruce: Digging Deeper > Robert the Bruce
Click on different topic headings to find out more.

We will never submit...

After the victory at Bannockburn, when the English had fled, even his Scottish enemies accepted that Bruce was now the rightful King of the Scots. In their eyes, Bruce's victory in battle showed that God was on his side.

However Edward II refused to give up his claim to be the overlord of Scotland. He sent an **envoy** to the Pope in Rome. As leader of the Church, the Pope could recognize Bruce as the ruler of a free kingdom. The English envoy reminded the Pope that Bruce had killed one of his enemies inside a church. In 1319 the Pope refused to accept Bruce as king, and ordered all priests in Scotland not to baptize, bury or marry any of Bruce's subjects.

Bruce met with his nobles and the Scottish bishops at Arbroath Abbey. They wrote three letters to Pope John explaining that Scotland was a separate kingdom from England and had a long history as a free nation.

The third letter, known as the Declaration of Arbroath, stated that Scotland was not part of England and had been invaded by Edward. However, the Scots had fought for their own liberty, not just for the rights of Robert the Bruce. King Robert was their leader but only for as long as he respected Scotland's freedom. If he accepted the English as overlords, the Scots would choose another king.

 Although now a ruin, Arbroath Abbey was one of the most important churches in Scotland at the time of Robert the Bruce.

In 1324 Pope John finally recognized Bruce as King of the Scots. The English signed a peace treaty in 1328 giving up any rights to Scotland. When Robert the Bruce died in 1329, his son David became king despite English support for another pretender – Edward Balliol. The conflict rumbled on for years afterwards, with the English actually forcing David into exile and placing Balliol on the throne in 1333.

The Battle of Bannockburn was one of the first times in history that common people defeated heavily armoured knights in battle. The Declaration of Arbroath was one of the first documents written by a free people to explain the idea of liberty. The wars had brought the people of Scotland together and made them united.

From the Declaration of Arbroath, 1320

"For as long as one hundred of us remain alive, we will never submit to rule by the English. For it is not for glory, riches or honour that we fight, but for freedom alone, which no good man will give up except with his life."

Exploring further – Written evidence

Much of our information about history comes from things that were written at the time, like the Declaration of Arbroath. The Written Sources section of the CD-ROM contains lots of different types of writing that tell us about the Middle Ages.

The Black Death in Scotland

King Robert died in 1329. Some historians think that he had leprosy, a terrible wasting disease that rots the body. Most people in the Middle Ages believed that God gave power to kings to heal the sick. One of King Robert's tasks was to lay his hands on the sick people who came to his court at Dunfermline. He may have caught this horrible disease when he was trying to heal the lepers in his kingdom.

Twenty years after the death of 'Good King Robert', a much more terrible disease spread across Scotland. This was the bubonic plague or the **Black Death**. The disease soon spread from the East to Europe on the ships of spice **merchants** trading in Venice. It reached England in the summer of 1349, killing tens of thousands within days.

At first the Scots thought that God was punishing their English enemies. It seemed a good time to invade England and try to recapture lost lands. A large Scottish army gathered at Selkirk near the border and prepared to attack. However some of the Scottish troops fell ill and showed signs of the plague. They fled back to their homes, carrying the infection to every part of the kingdom.

Swelling under the arms and large spots on the skin were just some of the terrible effects of the Black Death on its victims.

A Scottish prayer from 1349 translated into English

"God and Saint Andrew, Saint Mungo and Saint Ninian, shield us this and every day from the foul death that the Englishmen are dying from."

Bubonic plague was a painful killer. Victims had large swellings under their arms that filled with pus and blood. There was no known cure and thousands suffered a slow, lingering death. Historians think that the plague killed over a third of the population. The death toll was highest in the **burghs** such as Aberdeen and Perth where the infection spread easily in the crowded streets.

Most Scots thought that God had sent the sickness, so they prayed to the saints for help. The burgh councils tried to fight the disease in other ways. The burghs were closed to strangers and Constables stood at the gates. People from parishes where the disease was strong were forbidden to enter on pain of death. The dead were buried in vast pits and their clothes destroyed in fires. Slowly the great sickness passed, leaving Scotland an emptier, sadder land.

 In some burghs, so many people died from the Black Death that it was difficult to bury them all properly.

Exploring further – Medieval medicine

Diseases like the Black Death were able to spread quickly because medieval ideas about illness were very basic. You can read about them on the CD-ROM. Follow this path: Exploring the Wider World > Focus On: Britain 1066–1500 > Disease and medicine.

Somerled and the Lords of the Isles

Throughout the Middle Ages, the Kingdom of the Scots ended where the mountains began. In the north and west of the country, the King of the Scots in far away Dunfermline had little power. Here there were other princes in command. Somerled was the first 'Lord of the Isles'. He had **Norse** and Irish blood in his veins and spoke **Gaelic**, the ancient language of Alba.

By 1140, Somerled had built a sea-kingdom that stretched throughout the islands of the west coast. He hated the growing influence of the noble **Norman** families who were changing southern Scotland. In 1164 he gathered a vast fleet of 160 **birlinns** or war-galleys, and sailed into the Firth of Clyde. His army **besieged** the castle at Renfrew. During the siege Somerled mysteriously died. Some historians think that one of his servants was bribed by the Normans to murder him. Without their leader, the Gaelic war-fleet sailed back home.

By 1400 the MacDonald princes ruled most of the islands. The MacDonald Lords held their court at Finlaggan Palace on Islay, and ordered their council to meet there. Every island sent representatives to discuss taxes and law cases about stolen land and goods.

 Castle Stalker in Lorn was defended by its high tower, raised entrance and the surrounding sea.

Above all, the Lords of the Isles enjoyed war and raiding the lowlands of the Scots. In 1411 a Highland army under Donald MacDonald even tried to capture the rich **burgh** of Aberdeen. Many of the Highland troops were the feared **gallowglasses** or mercenaries who fought with the long **Lochaber axe**. They were stopped at the bloody battle of Harlaw near Inverurie.

The most powerful Highland lord was John MacDonald who became Lord of the Isles in 1449. He built up his army and fleet and plotted to defeat the King of the Scots. He even wrote to the English King Edward IV to suggest an alliance. Edward and MacDonald planned to attack the Kingdom of the Scots at the same time and divide it in two.

 From a Scottish chronicle written in 1450

"The warlike Donald of the Isles ravaged the land and went to sack the burgh of Aberdeen and then bring the whole country to the Tay under his power."

Eventually in 1493, James IV acted to protect the Kingdom of Scotland from this troublesome rival. James set out from Newark Castle near Greenock to crush the MacDonalds. Their power or Lordship over the Isles was abolished. Nevertheless the Highlands and islands remained distant and separate from the rest of the kingdom.

Exploring further – Other civilizations

Try comparing Scotland in the Middle Ages to a civilization on another continent. The CD-ROM explores the Aztec civilization of central America:
Exploring the Wider World > Focus On: The Aztecs
Remember that America was not even discovered by Europeans until 1492.

Life in a lowland toun

By 1350 most people in lowland Scotland lived in small villages called touns. Usually five or six families lived and worked together in a toun. The toun's folk lived in longhouses with one end given over to the animals. The houses were often surrounded by a low earth wall. Inside the wall were **byres** for storing feed, and pens for smaller animals such as pigs and chickens.

There were some bad years when the weather was poor and the harvest was disappointing. Invading English armies sometimes burnt crops and stole food. However, the people of Scotland were usually well fed. Everyone lived close to the land or to the sea, so there was almost always enough food to go round.

Oats and barley were the main foods that everyone ate. They were crops that thrived in Scotland's damp soil. Most Scots ate oats and barley every day as porridge, oatmeal or barley bannocks. Mutton, cheese and milk came from sheep and goats. There was no shortage of fish and other seafood. Most people, including children, drank ale made from barley and honey.

A comment by an Italian traveller to Scotland in 1435

"The common people of Scotland stuff themselves with large amounts of mutton and fish and look on bread as a delicacy."

Scottish peasants were experts at making food last. Dishes like haggis were invented to make use of every part of their animals.

Wool was very important; it was used to make clothes of rough brown and grey cloth. **Merchants** came round every year and bought up any extra. Sheep were a common sight, especially in the rich Border lands. Many of the flocks were owned by the monks who ran the Border abbeys. In the 1370s the **burgh** of Berwick sent over two million fleeces to Europe.

Most lowland Scots were freeborn but some were peasants called **neyfs**. The local lord gave them land to farm for themselves, but the neyfs had to spend most of their time working on the lord's estate. They were forbidden to leave the land without their lord's permission. If the lord sold the land, the neyfs were sold with it. By 1400 most neyfs had earned their freedom. After the **Black Death**, landowners had to pay labourers to do hard farming tasks.

Neyfs on Border estates were skilled in the art of husbanding sheep. Many made their living from the wool trade between the Borders and Europe.

Exploring further – Searching the Middle Ages

To find more information about the Middle Ages click on Search on the top panel of the Contents page. Pick a word from the keywords on the next page and click on Enter. The screen will now show a list of pages on the CD-ROM that mention this word. Click on the names of the pages to find out what they show.

Timeline

AD 1000   First large trading settlements established at river mouths

1018   Strathclyde becomes part of kingdom of Alba/Scotia

1040   First **Normans** settle in Scotland

1058   Malcolm Canmore follows Macbeth as king

1070   Malcolm marries Margaret.
Dunfermline Abbey founded by Queen Margaret.

1124   David I becomes king – founds over 60 royal **burghs**

1138   Somerled becomes Lord of the Hebrides

1249   Alexander III becomes king

1286   Alexander dies in a fall at Kinghorn cliffs

1290   Death of Margaret of Norway in Orkney

1292   King Edward of England chooses John Balliol to be king of Scotland

1295   Balliol refuses to obey Edward

1296   Edward invades and conquers Scotland

1297   Wallace and Murray rise in rebellion against Edward

1298   Wallace defeated at Falkirk and flees to Europe

1305   Wallace handed over to Edward – tortured and executed

1306   Robert the Bruce crowns himself King of the Scots

1307   Bruce defeated at battles of Methven and Dalry

1308   Bruce ravages the lands of Buchan

1314   Bruce defeats Edward II at the Battle of Bannockburn

1320   Declaration of Arbroath

1328   Treaty of Edinburgh

1329   Death of Robert the Bruce

1350   **Black Death** reaches Scotland

1411   MacDonald's army attacks Aberdeenshire

1493   James IV abolishes the Lordship of the Isles

Glossary

archaeologist   scientist who finds and examines evidence from the past

beseige   surround an enemy castle, to starve them into surrendering

birlinn   war-galley based on Norse warships used by the Gaelic peoples of the Hebrides

Black Death   great plague that swept across Europe between 1346 and 1350

brecbannoch   jewelled silver box which contained the holy bones of St Columba

burghs   market towns established across Scotland by David I in the 12th century

byre   barns for sheltering animals and storing crops over the winter

civil war   war in which both sides are from the same people or country

clachan   Gaelic word for a small fermtoun or farming village

Deacon   burgh guild-master in charge of apprentices and enforcing the rules of his guild

envoy   ambassador or messenger who carries a message to a foreign king or leader

Gaelic   original language of the Scots, replaced by Scots English during the later Middle Ages

gallowglasses   feared mercenary troops from Ireland and the Highlands specializing in using battleaxes

Great Hall   main room of a castle used for banquets and other important occasions

guild   craftsmen who banded together to set prices and make sure that only high quality goods were sold in their burgh

Lochaber axe   long handled axe with a blade on one side and a curved hook on the other, used for pulling men off horses

mason   expert builder in stone who could build castles and cathedrals

Mercat Cross   stone pillar marking the spot where burgh merchants were allowed to sell their wares

merchants   traders who made their living by buying and selling

neyf   Scottish name for serf or farm labourer who had to work on their master's land and obey him

Normans   powerful warriors from northern France who conquered England in 1066

Norse   raiders and settlers in northern Scotland and the islands, who came from Norway after 800

pilgrims   travellers who went on long journeys to important religious places such as the holy shrine at St Andrews

Provost   most important official on a burgh council in charge of keeping law and order in the town

scriptorium   room in a monastery where monks copied ancient books

stockade   fence of sharpened wooden stakes used as part of the defences of a burgh

toft   land at the rear of a burgh house where the householder could keep animals or grow vegetables

treasurer   officer in charge of the king's money and collecting taxes

Tron   public weighing scales used to make sure that merchants were not cheating their customers

Index

Titles in the *Explore Scottish History* series include:

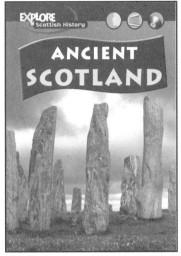

Hardback   0 431 14520 2

Hardback   0 431 14522 9

Hardback   0 431 14524 5

Hardback   0 431 14526 1

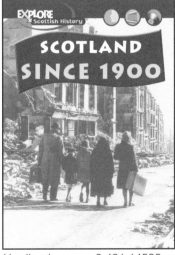

Hardback   0 431 14530 x

Find out about the other titles in this series on our website www.heinemann.co.uk/library